Just My Thoughts and Feelings

Chelsea Gray

BookLeaf Publishing

India | USA | UK

Just My Thoughts and Feelings © 2022
Chelsea Gray

All rights reserved.

Presentation by *BookLeaf Publishing*

Web: www.bookleafpub.com

E-mail: info@bookleafpub.com

ISBN: 9789357446501

First edition 2022

I'm Scared

I'm scared.

I'm scared of what the future holds

I'm scared I'm not ready to move out

I'm scared I won't get a job

I'm scared I won't finish my book

I'm just scared.

But

I know the future can be exciting

I know I'll move out and be okay

I know I'll get a job, even if I don't like it

I know I'll finish my book

And many more

All I can do for now is take the steps

To make my future a reality

I will do anything I set my mind to

Even if I'm scared.

My House Is Too Loud

My house is too loud

I can not focus here

There's jazz and Jazz

And stomping

And TVs

And video games

It's just so loud

I miss the partial silence

The sounds of papers flipping

Keyboards typing

All alone but not completely

I crave a desk and a chair

Ready to study

I don't have that here

I used to be so productive

Now I just procrastinate productively

All this changed so fast

My house is too loud but

Maybe I can use this noise for good

I just need it to be a bit quieter

I know I can do this

I've done it before

That Sounds Stresful

That sounds stressful
Because it is
I just need a minute
A minute to breath
To think
To just be
I don't want to
Be worried
About upcoming events
I want to be excited
I don't want to be stressed
I want to be relaxed
But for now
I'll just keep stealing moments
Taking time to myself
Faking it
Until I'm not stressed

I'm Just Tired

Honestly, I'm tired
Tired of working
Being ignored
Being alone
Just tired
I know I work hard
For my future
But when will
My future be
My present
When won't I be tired

I wish

I wish you saw you
The way I see you
I see a strong person
A capable person
Someone who
Is more than enough
Someone who
Deserves the world
But a better one
Than we have
You be you
I believe in you
No matter what

My Pen Glides

As my pen glides across
A fresh sheet of paper
I'm reminded of simpler times
Quieter days
As my pen glides across
A sheet of paper
I reflect on what is
And what could have been

I Believe

I believe there's always room to grow
I believe no one is perfect
I believe in myself
I believe in you
I know life is hard
But when you have something
To believe in
Or someone to believe in
That makes it all worth it

There's Always One

There's always one
One person that goes
Against everything
One that thinks
They're always right
There's always one
That can make a change
That can inspire people
Be that one

Some People

Some people make it so hard to help them
Some people just won't accept it
Some people don't know how to help
Some people are so hard to help
Some people just can't be helped
But help is always there
Whether offered or asked for
It's always there

Dementia

Chelsea, did you graduate?
Yes
And you didn't go to the graduation?
No
Silence

Chelsea, how's school going?
Good
When do you graduate?
Hopefully soon
Silence

It hurts to see this
To be part of it
And there's nothing we can do
Just watch and wait

I Love...

I love that something
Is always in the last
Place you look
That things are not
Always as they seem

I love that everyone
Should expect
The unexpected
But no one does

I love that life is this
Crazy mess of events
And we just accept it for
What it is and think
Nothing of it

I love that there's
So many different
Ways to experience the
Same day
And you won't get the
same day twice

I love what life is

What it could be
What it will be
What it was
It's just so
Fascinating

I'm Not Alone

Being lonely is the worst
But even worse is
Knowing you're not alone
But still feeling like you are
Sometimes, at that point
I'd rather be alone
But being lonely sucks

Choice

It's the choice
that matters
Being able to choose
who you are
what you feel
That's what I love

Being told
who you are
or
what you feel
shouldn't be a thing
It's my life
Let me live it
how I want

Mornings Be Like

I'm not really a morning person
I just fake it until I fully wake up
Like I'm on auto pilot all morning
I say mornings are evil
And they are
People like to
Ask me questions
First thing in the morning
I'm not even fully awake yet
I just fake it until I wake up

Drinking Coffee Makes Me Human

Drinking coffee, feeling human
The warmth is comforting
The sugar exciting
Coffee is my lifeline
It helps me pass
As a functioning adult
Drinking coffee makes me feel human
I need my caffiene IV
Twice a day
The smell of a fresh
Cup of coffee
Gets me up
In the morning
And the afternoon
Coffee makes me feel alive

"Columbus" Day

Do we have columbus day off?
Honestly, we should.
Right. It is after all
The day this great nation
Was "discovered"
We should celebrate all the deaths
Caused by Christopher Columbus
One mistake changed the fate
Of so, so many people.
So yea, we should have the day off
To remember and learn
About the Native Americans
That were killed

It Hurts Me

When you're silent
It hurts me
I can't keep asking
If you're okay
I just get the
Same response
But different words
I get I'm fine
Yea
I'm good
But your eyes say
Differently
They're asking for help
I'm here for you
Just let me in

Running

Running
out of space
out of time
out of everything
why can't anything
just stay still
not forever
but
maybe five minutes
or at least
until I
have my shit
together
I'm tired
of chasing
can I just
stop running
chasing things
everything should stop
then restart
time, space
everything
just
stop
running

Me

they call me smart

but I don't care

they call me a genius

I still don't care

they say I'm mean

there's no proof

they say I'm crazy

there's still no proof

I say I'm lazy

but smart

I say I'm crazy

but in a good way

I know I'm awesome

but don't care

I know I'm weird

but I'm me

Trends

Anything can become a trend
Why?
Are we really that bored that
we are willing to get random
people and things trending?
People wake up every morning
first thing they do
check Twitter to see
what's trending
Why?
What happened to the time
when people would wake up
and sit at the kitchen
table and read
not our timelines
not our news feeds
but a newspaper
they are still delivered but
no one reads them
Why?
"social" networks are making us
less social
each update takes us further
away from people
each new "social" app

is making us less social
the current trend:
#what'sthenexttrend
it should be:
<- this is a pound symbol
and putting down the phone and tablet
and turning off the computer
instead, it's all about
who is doing what
who is wearing what
and did you see what
so and so just posted
Why?
when did # <- this
go from meaning
pound to meaning
hashtag
when was the last time
you hung out with friends
and didn't check your phone
or use your phone
Twitter, Instagram, Facebook
they are destroying what
we are really about
#i'mdonewiththisworld
hashtag needs to stop
trends need to stop
everything needs to stop
people need to take a step

back and look at their lives
where they were
where they are going
where they are now
we should all just stop
step back
and look
at what we have become
because of trends